The Super Librarians and The Trial of Fury

Summary

Chapter 1: The Evolution of Librarianship

From Book Guardians to Information Navigators

The role of librarians has undergone a profound transformation from the traditional custodians of books to dynamic information navigators. In the past, librarians were often perceived as gatekeepers of knowledge, with their primary responsibilities revolving around the acquisition, cataloging, and lending of physical books. However, as society entered the information age, these roles expanded significantly.

Librarians have become adept at guiding patrons through an ever-expanding digital landscape. They are no longer merely curators of content but also educators who teach information literacy skills. This shift necessitates that librarians possess a deep understanding of how to evaluate sources for credibility and relevance in an era where misinformation proliferates.

One example is the initiative taken by many libraries to host workshops on media literacy and critical thinking. These programs empower community members to discern fact from fiction in news articles and social media posts. Librarians lead these sessions, drawing upon their expertise in research methodologies and source evaluation.

Furthermore, librarians have embraced the role of technology specialists. Many are proficient in using digital databases, e-books, and online archives. They assist patrons with navigating complex search engines and utilizing software for various projects. This technological fluency is essential for modern librarianship as it ensures equitable access to information across diverse populations.

In addition to these skills, librarians have become community connectors who facilitate discussions on important societal issues. They organize book clubs that delve into topics such as social justice or environmental sustainability, fostering a culture of lifelong learning and civic engagement.

For further reading on this evolution, "Participatory Culture in a Networked Era" by Henry Jenkins et al., provides insights into how digital cultures can be navigated effectively—a skill set that today's librarians must master.

The Digital Transformation of Libraries

The digital transformation of libraries is one of the most significant shifts within librarian practice over recent decades. The advent of the internet and digital technologies has revolutionized how libraries function and serve their communities.

Digital collections now complement—and sometimes even replace—physical ones. Libraries offer access to vast arrays of e-books, audiobooks, academic journals, and multimedia resources that can be accessed remotely 24/ 7.

This convenience has democratized access to knowledge like never before; however, it also presents challenges such as ensuring digital preservation and combating the digital divide.

Libraries have responded by becoming more than just places to borrow materials; they are now vibrant community centers equipped with computer labs, makerspaces equipped with 3D printers and other tools for creative exploration, as well as spaces for teleconferencing that cater to remote learners or professionals.

An illustrative case study is the San Antonio Public Library system which launched BiblioTech—the first all-digital public library in the United States—in 2013.

It offers residents access to thousands of e-books and audiobooks without a single physical book on site. This innovative model demonstrates how libraries can adapt their services in response to changing technological landscapes while still fulfilling their mission.

To explore more about this topic "BiblioTech: Why Libraries Matter More Than Ever in the Age of Google" by John Palfrey provides an excellent overview of why embracing digital technology is crucial for libraries' survival in modern society.

Embracing New Roles in the Information Age

In embracing new roles within the information age, librarians are redefining what it means to be an information professional. Their work extends beyond traditional library walls into realms such as data management, open-access advocacy, intellectual property rights education, and even social media curation.

One emerging role is that of data librarian—a specialist who helps researchers manage large datasets effectively throughout research cycles. Data librarians play a crucial part in ensuring data integrity and accessibility which is vital for reproducibility in scientific research.

Another area where librarians are making strides is advocating for open access publishing models which aim at removing paywalls so that scholarly work can reach wider audiences without financial barriers—a move towards democratizing academic knowledge production.

Moreover, some librarians have taken up positions within corporate environments where they apply their expertise in managing internal knowledge bases or conducting competitive intelligence research—demonstrating versatility within various sectors outside traditional library settings.

A notable example includes initiatives like Mozilla's Open Leaders program which trains individuals—including many librarians—in open practices designed to foster collaboration and innovation across disciplines including technology development and scientific research. For those interested in exploring these new frontiers further "Open Access" by Peter Suber offers comprehensive insight into one aspect where modern-day librarians are leading change within scholarly communication systems.

In conclusion...

Each section above delves deeper into how modern-day librarians navigate through evolving landscapes—from being guardians of books to becoming versatile information navigators adept at handling both analog artifacts and digital interfaces; from adapting physical spaces into digitally integrated hubs; to taking on new roles that reflect broader societal shifts towards openness and inclusivity within knowledge ecosystems. As we continue witnessing rapid advancements across technological platforms coupled with complex socio-political dynamics shaping our world today—it becomes increasingly clear why we need super-librarians more than ever before: To guide us through this intricate maze ensuring truth prevails over noise while championing free access for all seekers after wisdom wherever they may be found.

Chapter 2: Battling Misinformation and Digital Fury

Understanding Misinformation in the Modern World

In the modern world, misinformation has become a pervasive force, shaping public opinion and influencing behaviors on a global scale. The advent of digital technology and social media platforms has exponentially increased the speed and reach of information dissemination, making it easier for false narratives to spread unchecked. Misinformation can range from innocent inaccuracies to deliberate disinformation campaigns designed to manipulate or deceive.

The roots of misinformation are complex and multifaceted. They include cognitive biases that predispose individuals to believe information that aligns with their pre-existing beliefs or emotions. Social networks amplify these effects by creating echo chambers where users are exposed primarily to viewpoints similar to their own, reinforcing their beliefs without challenge. Additionally, the sheer volume of information available online makes it difficult for individuals to discern credible sources from unreliable ones.

Misinformation can have serious consequences, from undermining democratic processes to endangering public health during crises like pandemics. For instance, during the COVID-19 pandemic, misinformation about the virus's origins, prevention methods, and treatments proliferated across social media platforms, leading to confusion and harmful behaviors.

To understand how misinformation spreads in the modern world, one must consider factors such as algorithmic amplification on social media platforms where sensational content is often prioritized over factual accuracy. Moreover, political actors and interest groups may engage in astroturfing—creating an illusion of grassroots support for particular viewpoints—to sway public opinion or policy decisions.

Real-world examples abound: The "Pizzagate" conspiracy theory that falsely linked high-profile politicians with a child trafficking ring led a man to fire shots inside a Washington D.C., pizzeria. This incident underscores how online falsehoods can translate into real-world violence.

Strategies for Combating Fake News and Propaganda

Combating fake news and propaganda requires a multi-pronged approach involving education, technology solutions, regulatory frameworks, and individual critical thinking skills. Media literacy education is crucial; by teaching people from an early age how to evaluate sources critically and check facts before sharing content online, society can build resilience against misinformation.

Technology companies play a pivotal role in this battle as they develop algorithms that prioritize credible content while demoting or removing false information. Artificial intelligence tools are increasingly being used to detect deepfakes—highly realistic manipulated videos—and other forms of sophisticated disinformation.

Collaboration between tech companies and fact-checking organizations has proven effective in identifying fake news stories quickly so they can be labeled or removed before they go viral. For example, Facebook's partnership with independent fact-checkers under its third-party fact-checking program helps reduce the spread of false stories on its platform.

Regulatory measures also contribute significantly by holding platforms accountable for the content they host without infringing on free speech rights—a delicate balance that continues to evolve through legal challenges and policy debates worldwide.

Individual actions matter too; encouraging critical thinking skills among internet users helps them question sensational headlines or dubious claims before accepting them as truth. Anecdotes such as the story of a group of students who created a website publishing outrageous but believable stories illustrate how easily people can be fooled if they do not verify information independently.

Librarians at the Forefront of Information Integrity

Librarians have emerged as unsung heroes in maintaining information integrity amidst an onslaught of misinformation. Their expertise extends far beyond traditional library services; librarians today are educators, technologists, community leaders, and defenders of intellectual freedom.

Their role involves curating collections with reliable resources across various formats—from books to databases—and guiding patrons toward accurate information while respecting diverse perspectives. Librarians also conduct workshops on media literacy where participants learn about evaluating sources' credibility using criteria such as authority, accuracy, currency, relevance, purpose/point-of-view (the CRAAP test).

Moreover, librarians actively participate in digital preservation efforts ensuring future generations have access to historical records untainted by revisionism or loss due to technological obsolescence—a vital aspect considering how easily digital records can be altered or deleted compared with physical documents.

Case studies highlight librarians' impact: In one instance during an election cycle when misleading political ads were rampant online; librarians set up "truth booths" providing voters with nonpartisan fact-checked information about candidates' positions on key issues.

In conclusion:

Understanding Misinformation in the Modern World: To navigate today's complex informational landscape effectively requires recognizing both psychological tendencies towards confirmation bias and technological mechanisms that facilitate rapid dissemination regardless of veracity.

Strategies for Combating Fake News and Propaganda: A comprehensive strategy encompassing education initiatives promoting media literacy alongside technological innovations aimed at detecting falsities offers hope against disinformation's tide. Librarians at the Forefront of Information Integrity: As custodians of knowledge committed to intellectual freedom principles; librarians stand out as essential allies fostering informed communities capable of discerning truth amid noise. For further reading on these topics consider "This Is Not Propaganda" by Peter Pomerantsev which explores contemporary manipulation techniques within global politics; "The Death Of Expertise" by Tom Nichols examining societal trends towards rejecting established knowledge authorities; "Factfulness" by Hans Rosling offering insights into why humans misinterpret data about world events despite evidence contrary perceptions; Lastly "The Information Literacy User's Guide" edited by Deborah Bernnard et al., provides practical guidance developing critical evaluation skills necessary today's digital environment.

Chapter 3: Research, Fact-Checking, and Critical Thinking

Developing Advanced Research Skills

In the realm of information science, developing advanced research skills is akin to mastering the art of navigation in a sea of data. It requires an understanding of not only where to look but also how to discern the quality and relevance of information found. In this context, librarians are often seen as the seasoned captains who guide others through tumultuous waters.

To cultivate these skills, one must first become adept at utilizing a variety of research tools and databases. This includes academic journals, specialized search engines, and digital libraries that offer access to peer-reviewed articles, books, and other scholarly materials. However, advanced research goes beyond mere access; it involves strategic searching techniques such as Boolean logic, keyword selection, and subject heading searches.

Moreover, researchers must be able to critically evaluate sources for credibility and bias. This involves examining the author's credentials, publication date, citations, and potential conflicts of interest. Understanding the methodology behind studies or experiments is crucial in assessing their validity.

Real-world examples demonstrate the importance of these skills. For instance, when researching historical events like the 1918 influenza pandemic, a librarian would not only seek primary sources from that period but also analyze recent interpretations by historians to provide patrons with a comprehensive view.

For further reading on developing advanced research skills, "The Craft of Research" by Wayne C. Booth et al., offers valuable insights into creating effective research strategies.

The Art of Fact-Checking in a Post-Truth Era

Fact-checking has always been an essential part of disseminating accurate information; however, its significance has been magnified in what many refer to as the post-truth era—a time characterized by misinformation and fake news. The role librarians play in this landscape is more critical than ever as they stand on the front lines defending factual integrity.

The art of fact-checking involves several layers: verifying facts against multiple reputable sources; understanding context; recognizing satire or parody; identifying logical fallacies; and being aware of deepfakes or manipulated media content. Librarians must be equipped with digital literacy skills that enable them to navigate these complexities effectively.

One poignant example is during election seasons when misinformation can sway public opinion significantly. Librarians can help patrons discern between legitimate political platforms and propaganda by guiding them towards non-partisan resources like government databases or fact-checking websites such as Snopes or FactCheck.org.

In addition to traditional methods, new technologies have emerged to assist with fact-checking efforts—artificial intelligence programs designed to detect falsehoods in text or image verification tools that trace origins of photographs online.

For those interested in delving deeper into this topic "The Truth Matters: A Citizen's Guide to Separating Facts from Lies and Stopping Fake News in Its Tracks" by Bruce Bartlett provides practical advice on navigating today's complex informational environment.

Fostering Critical Thinking Among Patrons

Critical thinking is an indispensable skill for any individual seeking to navigate life's myriad challenges thoughtfully and effectively. Libraries serve as incubators for this skill set by providing resources that encourage analysis, synthesis, evaluation—and ultimately—understanding.

Librarians foster critical thinking among patrons through various means: curated book displays on controversial topics invite exploration from multiple perspectives; organized debates or discussion groups stimulate intellectual engagement; workshops on media literacy empower individuals with tools for discernment; while personalized reference services guide users toward thoughtful inquiry rather than passive consumption.

An anecdote illustrating this might involve a librarian assisting a high school student researching climate change. By presenting both scientific literature and socio-political commentary on environmental policy decisions alongside each other—the librarian encourages nuanced consideration rather than one-dimensional reasoning.

Furthermore, libraries often collaborate with educational institutions offering courses specifically designed to enhance critical thinking abilities—such as philosophy or ethics classes—which are open for community members' participation too.

For those wishing to explore further how libraries contribute towards cultivating critical thinkers amongst their patronage "Critical Library Pedagogy Handbook" edited by Nicole Pagowsky & Kelly McElroy provides comprehensive strategies employed within library instruction programs worldwide.

Chapter 4: Promoting Literacy and Lifelong Learning

Literacy Initiatives and Reading Programs

In the realm of literacy initiatives and reading programs, librarians have emerged as pivotal figures in crafting innovative strategies to foster a love for reading across all age groups. These initiatives are not just about teaching individuals to read but also about nurturing an environment where reading is seen as a valuable and enjoyable activity. One such initiative is the integration of technology with traditional reading practices. E-books, audiobooks, and interactive storytelling apps have become tools in the librarian's arsenal to attract tech-savvy generations back to literature.

Reading programs often target specific demographics, such as early childhood reading hours that encourage parents to read with their children, fostering early language development and bonding. For school-aged children, summer reading challenges with incentives can help prevent the 'summer slide' in literacy skills. Teen book clubs might focus on young adult fiction that deals with contemporary issues, providing a safe space for discussion and exploration.

Adults are not left out of these initiatives; many libraries offer adult literacy programs aimed at those who may have slipped through the educational cracks or non-native speakers seeking to improve their language skills. Moreover, libraries often host author events and book signings which serve as both community-building events and opportunities for readers to engage deeply with literature.

Libraries also recognize the importance of inclusivity in their literacy efforts. They curate diverse collections that reflect various cultures, languages, and experiences ensuring that everyone sees themselves represented on the shelves. This diversity extends into programming too – from multilingual story times to literature festivals celebrating authors from minority backgrounds.

Engaging Diverse Audiences in Learning Activities

Engaging diverse audiences requires an understanding that learning is not one-size-fits-all. Libraries have become adept at recognizing the unique needs of different community segments and developing tailored learning activities that resonate with each group's interests and cultural backgrounds.

For instance, libraries may offer coding workshops for teens interested in technology or career-focused seminars for adults looking to upskill or change professions. They might also provide financial literacy workshops for low-income families or host citizenship classes for immigrants navigating the naturalization process.

To reach those who may be intimidated by formal education settings or who have had negative experiences in the past, libraries create informal learning environments that are welcoming and supportive. They employ hands-on learning methods like maker spaces where creativity is encouraged through DIY projects ranging from robotics to crafts.

Furthermore, libraries often go beyond their walls by setting up pop-up libraries in community centers, parks, or even shopping malls to reach people who might not typically visit a library building. Mobile libraries serve rural areas where access might be limited due to distance or lack of transportation.

Collaborations with Educational Institutions

The collaboration between libraries and educational institutions has opened new avenues for enhancing educational outcomes through shared resources, expertise, and programming. These partnerships range from joint research projects between universities and public libraries to shared catalog systems that allow students broader access to materials.

One significant area of collaboration involves information literacy instruction where librarians work alongside teachers to develop students' abilities to locate, evaluate, and use information effectively – a critical skill in today's digital world. Librarians bring their expertise into classrooms through guest lectures or co-teaching sessions designed around research-based assignments.

Another collaborative effort includes bridging gaps during transitional periods such as high school students preparing for college-level work or adults returning to education after time away. Libraries can offer specialized resources like test preparation materials or databases specifically geared towards academic research.

Moreover, collaborations extend into community engagement projects where students can participate in real-world problem-solving under the guidance of librarians – whether it's archiving local history or engaging in civic technology initiatives that benefit local communities.

In conclusion:

Each section above delves deeper into how modern librarians champion literacy initiatives while embracing technological advancements; engage diverse audiences through inclusive programming; collaborate with educational institutions; all aimed at promoting lifelong learning within communities they serve. For further exploration on these topics: - "Reading Unbound: Why Kids Need to Read What They Want—and Why We Should Let Them" by Jeffrey Wilhelm & Michael Smith - "Palaces for the People: How Social Infrastructure Can Help Fight Inequality" by Eric Klinenberg - "The New Literacies: Multiple Perspectives on Research and Practice" edited by Elizabeth A. Baker

These works provide additional insights into how we can continue supporting literacy development across various demographics while fostering an environment conducive to lifelong learning—a testament to the evolving role of librarians as guardians of knowledge within our society.

Chapter 5: Preserving History and Cultural Heritage

Archiving the Past: Techniques and Challenges

The process of archiving the past is a complex endeavor that involves preserving historical records, artifacts, and cultural heritage for future generations. Archivists employ various techniques to ensure that these materials remain accessible over time. One common method is the use of acid-free paper for documents and proper environmental controls to prevent deterioration of physical items. Digitization has also become a key technique in preservation, allowing for easier access and reducing the handling of fragile originals.

However, archiving faces numerous challenges. Physical degradation is an ever-present threat, with materials being susceptible to environmental factors such as light, temperature fluctuations, and humidity. Additionally, political instability can lead to the destruction or looting of archives. The digital realm introduces its own set of challenges; technological obsolescence can render digital formats unreadable within a few years if not properly managed.

Moreover, there's an ethical dimension to archiving: deciding what gets preserved and what doesn't can be subjective and reflect cultural biases. This selective memory can lead to gaps in history where marginalized voices are underrepresented or omitted entirely.

Real-world examples include the efforts to preserve ancient manuscripts in Timbuktu amidst political unrest or the digitization projects undertaken by the British Library to safeguard texts that date back centuries. These cases highlight both the fragility of historical records and the dedication required to protect them.

For further reading on this topic, "Archives: Principles and Practices" by Laura Millar provides an excellent overview of archival science and its contemporary challenges.

Digital Preservation Efforts

In response to the rapid advancement of technology, digital preservation has become a critical aspect of archiving history and cultural heritage. Digital preservation involves maintaining access to digital materials over time as original technologies become obsolete—a process known as 'bit rot.' To combat this issue, institutions often employ strategies like migration (transferring data from one system to another) or emulation (creating software that imitates older systems).

One significant effort in this field is LOCKSS (Lots Of Copies Keep Stuff Safe), which uses a decentralized model for preserving academic journals online by maintaining multiple copies across different locations. Another example is the Internet Archive's Wayback Machine, which captures snapshots of web pages over time so they can be accessed even after they have been altered or taken down.

Despite these efforts, digital preservation faces hurdles such as ensuring long-term readability of files due to changing software and hardware standards. There's also a financial cost associated with maintaining large-scale digital archives that must be considered.

A case study worth examining is the work done by The Digital Preservation Coalition (DPC), which provides resources and advocacy for digital preservation initiatives worldwide. Their handbook offers insights into best practices for sustaining our digital legacy.

For those interested in exploring more about this subject matter, "Understanding Digital Preservation: A Primer" by Daniel J. Gomes et al., offers a comprehensive look at methodologies used in preserving our digital world.

Showcasing Hidden Histories

Uncovering hidden histories involves bringing light to stories that have been overlooked or suppressed due to various reasons such as colonialism, racism, sexism, or other forms of discrimination. Librarians play a crucial role in showcasing these narratives through curated exhibitions, special collections focused on minority groups' contributions, oral history projects capturing personal accounts from diverse communities.

An example includes projects like "The HistoryMakers," which focuses on recording African American oral histories across various fields—ensuring their experiences are part of America's fabric. Similarly, initiatives like Europeana Collections provide access to millions of artworks from European museums with an emphasis on inclusivity regarding lesser-known artists or periods.

Challenges arise when attempting to showcase hidden histories because often there are limited primary sources available due either their destruction or never having been recorded initially due societal biases at those times against certain groups' contributions being deemed worthy documentation.

To delve deeper into how hidden histories are brought into public consciousness despite these obstacles consider reading "Silencing The Past: Power And The Production Of History" by Michel-Rolph Trouillot which explores mechanisms through which certain narratives become dominant while others fade into obscurity.

In conclusion each area presents unique opportunities insights into how we preserve interpret our collective pasts whether it be through traditional archival methods adapting new technologies uncovering stories previously untold all contribute towards richer more inclusive understanding human experience across time space As society continues evolve so too must approaches ensuring knowledge remains safeguarded accessible all who seek learn from it

Chapter 6: Emotional Neutrality in Service Delivery

Maintaining Professionalism Under Pressure

In the high-stakes environment of service delivery, maintaining professionalism under pressure is not just a desirable trait but a critical requirement. Professionals across various fields often encounter situations that test their composure and ability to perform effectively amidst stress. This challenge is particularly pronounced for those in customer-facing roles, where the pressure to maintain a calm and collected demeanor is compounded by the unpredictability of human interactions.

One key aspect of maintaining professionalism under pressure is emotional intelligence (EI). EI involves the capacity to be aware of, control, and express one's emotions judiciously and empathetically. It also encompasses the ability to handle interpersonal relationships with care. Professionals with high EI are better equipped to navigate stressful situations without allowing their emotions to dictate their responses.

Another crucial factor is the development of coping strategies. These can range from deep breathing techniques and mindfulness exercises to more structured approaches like cognitive-behavioral techniques that help individuals reframe negative thoughts into positive actions. Additionally, time management skills can alleviate work-related stress by helping professionals prioritize tasks and set realistic deadlines.

Real-world examples abound where maintaining professionalism has made a significant difference in outcomes. Consider air traffic controllers who must remain focused and clear-headed despite the life-or-death nature of their decisions or medical professionals who navigate emotionally charged environments daily while making critical care decisions.

For further reading on this topic, "Emotional Intelligence 2.0" by Travis Bradberry and Jean Greaves provides insights into developing emotional intelligence skills that can help maintain professionalism under challenging circumstances.

Training for Emotional Resilience

Emotional resilience refers to an individual's ability to adapt to stressful situations or crises. Training for emotional resilience equips service providers with tools and techniques necessary for bouncing back from setbacks and handling high-pressure scenarios effectively.

One approach to building emotional resilience is through regular training programs that include role-playing exercises designed to simulate stressful encounters. These simulations allow individuals to practice their responses in a controlled environment, which can reduce anxiety when faced with real-life challenges.

Mindfulness-based stress reduction (MBSR) programs have also gained popularity as a method for enhancing emotional resilience. MBSR teaches participants how to stay present in the moment without judgment, which can help mitigate feelings of overwhelm during intense situations.

Physical fitness should not be overlooked as part of resilience training either; there is substantial evidence linking physical health with mental well-being. Regular exercise has been shown to reduce symptoms of anxiety and depression while improving cognitive function—all essential components for dealing with stress effectively.

The military offers an example where comprehensive resilience training programs have been implemented successfully. Soldiers are trained not only physically but also psychologically, preparing them for the rigors they face both on and off the battlefield.

For those interested in exploring this area further, "The Resilience Factor" by Karen Reivich and Andrew Shatté provides practical advice on developing resilience skills that can be applied across various aspects of life.

Case Studies on Conflict Resolution

Conflict resolution plays a pivotal role in service delivery as it directly impacts customer satisfaction and retention. Effective conflict resolution requires a combination of communication skills, empathy, problem-solving abilities, and sometimes negotiation tactics.

Case studies offer valuable insights into successful conflict resolution strategies employed by organizations worldwide. For instance, consider how hospitality industry leaders train staff members in de-escalation techniques that turn potentially volatile guest complaints into opportunities for service recovery.

Another case study might examine how tech companies manage conflicts arising from product failures or service disruptions—often employing transparent communication channels like social media platforms or dedicated support teams trained specifically in crisis management protocols.

In healthcare settings, conflict resolution takes on added significance due to potential implications for patient safety and care quality. Here we find interdisciplinary teams working collaboratively using structured communication tools such as SBAR (Situation-Background-Assessment-Recommendation) which facilitate clear information exchange among caregivers thus preventing misunderstandings that could escalate into conflicts.

For readers seeking more detailed explorations into conflict resolution mechanisms within organizations "Getting To Yes: Negotiating Agreement Without Giving In" by Roger Fisher William Ury offers timeless principles on reaching mutually beneficial agreements even in adversarial negotiations.

Chapter 7: Ethical Considerations in Access to Information

Balancing Open Access with Privacy Concerns

In the digital age, the concept of open access to information has become a cornerstone of knowledge dissemination. However, this noble pursuit often clashes with the equally important need for privacy. The balance between these two principles is delicate and requires constant negotiation.

Open access initiatives aim to remove barriers to scholarly and educational resources, allowing for the democratization of knowledge. This movement has gained significant momentum, particularly in academia, where researchers advocate for unrestricted sharing of their work. The benefits are manifold: students and scholars from around the world can tap into vast repositories of knowledge that were previously behind paywalls or restricted by geography.

Yet, this openness can inadvertently expose personal data or sensitive information. In an era where data breaches are commonplace, protecting individuals' privacy becomes paramount. Libraries and information centers must navigate these waters carefully; they have a duty to both provide access to information and safeguard users' personal details.

One approach is implementing robust data protection policies that align with legal frameworks such as the General Data Protection Regulation (GDPR) in Europe. Another strategy involves anonymizing data before it's shared openly, ensuring that individuals cannot be identified from the datasets released.

Real-world examples abound where this balance has been tested. For instance, universities often grapple with whether to make thesis documents publicly available online—documents that may contain proprietary research or personal information about research subjects.

To further explore this topic, readers might delve into "Privacy and Freedom" by Alan Westin or "The Future of Ideas" by Lawrence Lessig. These works provide foundational insights into privacy rights and intellectual property in the context of open access.

Censorship vs Freedom of Information Debates

The tension between censorship and freedom of information is a battleground with deep historical roots that continue to grow in complexity as technology evolves. Censorship represents an attempt by governments, institutions, or other entities to suppress material deemed inappropriate or dangerous, while freedom of information advocates argue for minimal restrictions on content availability.

This debate often centers around who gets to decide what information should be censored for the greater good versus upholding an individual's right to access comprehensive unfiltered content. Proponents of censorship argue that certain materials can cause societal harm—such as hate speech inciting violence or false information leading to public health risks—and thus should be controlled.

On the other hand, freedom of information supporters contend that censorship infringes on fundamental human rights and stifles democratic discourse. They argue that individuals should have the autonomy to discern truth from falsehood and make informed decisions based on all available data.

A poignant case study is found in authoritarian regimes where government censorship restricts citizens' access to global news sources or social media platforms—a stark contrast to more liberal societies where such freedoms are protected but also abused through misinformation campaigns.

For those interested in delving deeper into this debate, books like "Free Speech: Ten Principles for a Connected World" by Timothy Garton Ash offer extensive analysis on free expression challenges in our interconnected society.

Protecting Users from Harmful Content

The responsibility of protecting users from harmful content falls heavily upon those who manage platforms where such content can proliferate—be it social media companies or libraries offering internet services. Harmful content ranges widely; it includes cyberbullying, graphic violence, extremist propaganda, pornography accessible by minors, and disinformation campaigns designed to deceive large populations.

Librarians play a crucial role here—they curate collections with an eye toward quality control while also respecting diverse viewpoints. They must walk a fine line between providing comprehensive resources and shielding patrons from potentially damaging material without encroaching on intellectual freedoms.

Digital literacy programs have emerged as one solution; they empower users with skills needed not only to identify credible sources but also protect themselves online against malicious content. Additionally, filters are sometimes employed within libraries' computer systems—though these tools are controversial due to their potential overreach blocking legitimate educational material alongside objectionable content.

An example highlighting these challenges occurred during the COVID-19 pandemic when librarians had to ensure their patrons could find accurate health information amidst a sea of misinformation about the virus circulating online.

Further reading on this subject could include "It's Complicated: The Social Lives of Networked Teens" by danah boyd which explores how young people interact with digital media and how adults can support them in navigating harmful content effectively.

Chapter 8: Technology Integration in Library Services

Adopting New Technologies for Enhanced Accessibility

In the realm of library services, adopting new technologies is not merely a matter of keeping up with trends; it's about breaking down barriers and enhancing accessibility for all patrons. The integration of assistive technologies such as screen readers, voice recognition software, and adjustable workstations has been pivotal in ensuring that libraries serve as inclusive spaces. However, the scope of technological adoption extends far beyond these tools.

One innovative example is the use of virtual reality (VR) to create immersive experiences for users with mobility issues or those who cannot physically visit the library. Through VR headsets, patrons can take virtual tours of historical sites or explore digital archives in a three-dimensional space, thus experiencing resources they might otherwise be unable to access.

Another significant advancement is the development of mobile applications tailored to library services. These apps often include features like text-to-speech and customizable font sizes and colors to accommodate users with visual impairments. Moreover, they provide remote access to library catalogs and e-resources, enabling users to interact with library services from any location at any time.

Libraries are also harnessing the power of artificial intelligence (AI) to enhance user accessibility. AI-driven chatbots can offer 24/7 assistance, answering queries and guiding users through online resources without human intervention. This technology ensures that help is available outside traditional opening hours, catering to those who may have time constraints or prefer digital communication.

The adoption of new technologies must be accompanied by staff training programs that enable librarians to assist patrons effectively in using these tools. Furthermore, libraries should engage in continuous dialogue with their communities to identify specific needs and tailor technological solutions accordingly.

For further reading on this topic, "Including Families of Children with Special Needs: A How-To-Do-It Manual for Librarians" by Carrie Scott Banks provides practical guidance on creating accessible library environments for diverse populations.

E-Libraries and Virtual Reference Services

The evolution of e-libraries and virtual reference services marks a transformative era in information retrieval and knowledge dissemination. E-libraries extend the reach of traditional brick-and-mortar institutions by providing digital collections that include e-books, academic journals, multimedia content, and databases accessible from anywhere at any time.

Virtual reference services complement e-libraries by offering real-time assistance through various channels such as email, chat interfaces, video calls, or social media platforms. These services cater to the immediacy of information needs in today's fast-paced world where users expect quick responses.

A case study worth examining is the Ask a Librarian service implemented by many libraries worldwide. This service allows patrons to receive personalized research assistance from professional librarians who can guide them through complex databases or recommend sources for their inquiries.

Moreover, collaborative networks among libraries have led to shared virtual reference services where expertise is pooled together across institutions— ensuring that even specialized queries receive accurate answers promptly.

As these services grow more sophisticated with advancements like AI-powered search algorithms and natural language processing capabilities, they promise an even more intuitive user experience. However, it's crucial that libraries maintain a balance between automated systems and human interaction to preserve the personal touch that is often appreciated by patrons seeking guidance.

For additional insights into this area's future direction, "Digital Reference Services" by R. David Lankes offers an extensive look at how technology shapes reference librarianship's principles and practices.

Data Management and Security Protocols

In an age where data breaches are increasingly common occurrences affecting all sectors—including libraries—robust data management and security protocols are non-negotiable elements within library operations. Libraries collect vast amounts of sensitive information ranging from personal patron data to proprietary research materials; hence safeguarding this data is paramount.

Effective data management begins with establishing clear policies regarding data collection practices—what information is necessary? How long should it be retained? Who has access? Answering these questions helps minimize risks associated with holding unnecessary data while ensuring compliance with privacy laws such as GDPR or CCPA.

Chapter 9: Redefining Library Spaces as Community Hubs

Designing Inclusive Spaces for Collaboration

In the realm of modern librarianship, the design of library spaces has evolved to meet the diverse needs of the community it serves. The creation of inclusive spaces for collaboration is a testament to this evolution. These spaces are not merely areas with tables and chairs; they are thoughtfully designed environments that encourage interaction, learning, and creativity among all members of society.

To achieve inclusivity, libraries must consider various factors such as accessibility, comfort, technology integration, and flexibility. Accessibility is paramount; every individual, regardless of physical ability or age, should be able to navigate and utilize the space without barriers. This includes wheelchair-accessible entrances and furniture, clear signage in multiple languages, and assistive technologies for those with visual or hearing impairments.

Comfort is another critical aspect. Libraries have introduced a variety of seating options to accommodate different preferences and activities—soft lounge chairs for reading, ergonomic workstations for computer use, and large tables that facilitate group projects or meetings. Natural lighting and noise control also play significant roles in creating an inviting atmosphere where patrons feel at ease.

Technology integration is essential in today's digital age. Libraries have become tech hubs offering high-speed internet access, multimedia production tools like 3D printers and recording studios, as well as collaborative software that allows users to share ideas seamlessly. By providing these resources, libraries empower users to engage in digital content creation rather than mere consumption.

Flexibility in space design ensures that libraries can adapt to various events and user needs. Movable furniture allows rooms to be reconfigured quickly for workshops or study groups. Quiet zones can be established for focused work while open areas may host lively discussions or performances.

Real-world examples abound where libraries have successfully implemented these principles. For instance, the Chicago Public Library's YOUmedia program provides teens with a dedicated space equipped with laptops, recording equipment, and mentorship opportunities—fostering collaboration among young creatives.

For further reading on designing inclusive library spaces that foster collaboration among diverse communities, "The Third Place: Inspiring Stories about the Great Good Places at the Heart of Our Communities" by Ray Oldenburg offers insights into creating public spaces that serve as community anchors.

Hosting Community Events and Workshops

Libraries have long been bastions of knowledge acquisition through books but hosting community events and workshops has transformed them into dynamic centers for experiential learning. These programs cater to a wide array of interests—from literacy classes to coding workshops—and serve as catalysts for community engagement.

When planning events or workshops, libraries must consider their audience's demographics and interests carefully. Programs should be diverse enough to appeal across ages, cultures, and socioeconomic backgrounds. For example, storytime sessions might be offered in multiple languages reflecting the community's linguistic diversity or financial literacy workshops could target different age groups with age-appropriate content.

Collaboration with local experts enhances the quality of these offerings. A library might partner with a local university professor to conduct a lecture series on climate change or team up with a chef from a popular restaurant to offer cooking classes featuring regional cuisine.

Promotion plays a crucial role in ensuring successful turnout for events. Libraries employ various marketing strategies including social media campaigns, partnerships with local schools or businesses who can help spread the word about upcoming events.

Anecdotes from successful events can inspire future programming decisions —for instance when patrons who attended a job fair hosted by their local library return months later to share how it helped them gain employment—this feedback validates efforts put into organizing such initiatives.

For those interested in exploring more about how libraries can effectively host community events and workshops that resonate with their patrons' needs while fostering lifelong learning experiences "Palaces for the People: How Social Infrastructure Can Help Fight Inequality," by Eric Klinenberg provides valuable insights into building social infrastructure through public institutions like libraries.

Building Partnerships with Local Organizations

The synergy between libraries and local organizations is pivotal in maximizing resources available within communities while enhancing service delivery by both parties involved. Partnerships range from collaborations with educational institutions which may provide expertise on certain subjects—to alliances with non-profits focusing on social issues relevant to local residents such as homelessness or food insecurity.

These partnerships often lead to innovative programs tailored specifically towards addressing community needs—for instance—a library might collaborate with a health clinic offering free screenings during an event focused on wellness education thereby providing immediate value alongside information dissemination.

Sustainability is key when building these relationships; therefore mutual benefits must be identified early on ensuring all parties remain committed over time rather than engaging in one-off projects without lasting impact. Case studies highlighting successful partnerships often reveal common themes such as shared goals clear communication channels regular evaluation processes— all contributing factors towards achieving desired outcomes whether they involve increasing literacy rates among children promoting cultural awareness through art exhibitions etcetera. For further exploration into how effective partnerships between libraries other organizations can enrich communities "Better Together: Restoring The American Community" by Robert D Putnam Lewis M Feldstein provides comprehensive analysis along practical advice cultivating strong networks within society's fabric. In conclusion each area discussed above represents integral components redefining library spaces beyond traditional confines becoming true hubs where knowledge meets action inspiration leads transformation individuals come together forming vibrant interconnected communities around globe celebrating intellectual freedom fighters everywhere emphasizing importance guardianship over noise chaos misinformation era ever-changing landscapes digital physical alike ensuring truth prevails always forevermore

Chapter10: Advocacy for Libraries in Public Policy

Lobbying for Sustainable Funding Models

The quest for sustainable funding models is a critical concern for libraries, as they strive to maintain and expand their services in the face of financial constraints. Libraries are not merely repositories of books but dynamic institutions that foster learning, provide access to technology, and serve as community centers. To ensure their survival and growth, librarians and library advocates must engage in strategic lobbying efforts aimed at securing long-term financial support from a variety of sources.

One approach to sustainable funding is the development of partnerships with local businesses and philanthropic organizations. By aligning library services with the interests of these partners, libraries can tap into new revenue streams. For instance, a library might collaborate with a tech company to offer coding workshops, which could be sponsored by the company as part of its corporate social responsibility initiatives.

Another avenue is advocating for legislation that provides dedicated funding for libraries. This could take the form of ballot measures or amendments that earmark a portion of local taxes specifically for library use. The success of such measures often hinges on effective campaigning and public education about the value libraries bring to communities.

Libraries also explore alternative funding models such as endowments, where private donations are invested, and the interest earned is used to fund library operations. This model provides a buffer against economic downturns and shifts in political priorities that can affect annual budgets.

In addition to these strategies, libraries are increasingly adopting entrepreneurial activities like hosting paid events, leasing space for private functions, or operating cafes within their premises. These ventures require careful planning to balance commercial activities with the core mission of providing free access to information.

To illustrate successful lobbying for sustainable funding models, one can look at the Seattle Public Library's 1998 campaign that led to voter approval of a $196.4 million bond measure for rebuilding its Central Library and renovating branches. This was achieved through extensive community outreach and clear communication about how the funds would be used.

In conclusion, lobbying for sustainable funding requires creativity, collaboration with stakeholders across sectors, legislative advocacy, and an entrepreneurial mindset among librarians. As they navigate this complex terrain, it's essential that they articulate a compelling vision of how libraries serve as vital resources in our society—now more than ever in an age dominated by digital information.

Libraries' Role in Education Policy Development

Libraries have long been recognized as pillars within educational ecosystems due to their role in promoting literacy and lifelong learning. However, their potential contribution extends far beyond these traditional boundaries into shaping education policy itself.

Librarians possess unique insights into how people interact with information—insights that are invaluable when developing policies aimed at enhancing educational outcomes across all age groups. They advocate for policies that integrate information literacy into school curricula from an early age so students can critically evaluate sources and navigate an increasingly complex information landscape.

Moreover, libraries act as testing grounds for innovative educational approaches due to their flexibility compared to formal classroom settings. Programs developed within libraries often address diverse learning styles and needs—providing valuable data on what works best before scaling up initiatives within schools or districts.

An example is the Chicago Public Library's YOUmedia program—a dedicated space where teens learn through making media projects—which has influenced broader discussions on incorporating maker spaces into school environments nationwide.

Furthermore, librarians contribute expertise on issues such as student privacy rights concerning digital resources used within schools—a growing concern given the proliferation of online learning tools.

In advocating for education policy development that reflects current realities while anticipating future needs, librarians must engage with policymakers at all levels—from local school boards to national government bodies—and build coalitions with educators, parents' groups, academic researchers, and other stakeholders who share common goals.

Concluding this section on education policy development: Libraries are not just adjuncts but active participants in crafting policies that shape our educational landscapes. Their involvement ensures policies are informed by practical experience coupled with foresight into evolving educational demands amid technological advancements.

Campaigns to Raise Public Awareness

Public awareness campaigns play a crucial role in highlighting the value libraries add to individuals' lives and communities at large. Such campaigns aim not only at increasing patronage but also at fostering deeper understanding among citizens about why supporting libraries is crucial—for democracy's health as much as individual enrichment.

Chapter11 : Leadership within the Library Profession

Cultivating Leadership Skills among Librarians

Leadership within the library profession is not merely a position but a process that involves continuous learning, growth, and the ability to inspire others. Cultivating leadership skills among librarians is essential for the evolution of libraries as dynamic institutions that can meet the challenges of an ever-changing information landscape. To foster these skills, it is crucial to understand that leadership can manifest in various roles, from library directors to front-line staff.

One effective approach to developing leadership skills is through formal education and training programs. These programs often focus on strategic planning, change management, communication skills, and advocacy. However, beyond structured learning environments, experiential learning opportunities such as project management or committee work provide practical experience in leading initiatives within the library context.

Moreover, embracing technology and innovation is a significant aspect of modern library leadership. Librarians must be adept at leveraging digital tools to enhance services and outreach. This includes understanding data analytics for informed decision-making and utilizing social media platforms for community engagement.

Another dimension of cultivating leadership is fostering a culture of inclusivity and diversity within libraries. Leaders must be equipped to create environments where diverse voices are heard and respected, which enriches the library's offerings and makes it more reflective of the community it serves.

Real-world examples include librarians who have led successful digital literacy campaigns or those who have spearheaded efforts to make libraries more accessible to marginalized populations. These leaders demonstrate how librarians can effect positive change both within their institutions and in their broader communities.

Mentorship Programs and Professional Development

Mentorship programs play a pivotal role in professional development for librarians by providing guidance, support, and opportunities for growth. Effective mentorship relationships can help new librarians navigate the complexities of their roles while also offering seasoned professionals a chance to give back to their community by sharing knowledge and expertise.

Professional development extends beyond mentorship; it encompasses attending conferences, workshops, webinars, and engaging with professional organizations. These activities keep librarians abreast of emerging trends, best practices, and innovative ideas that they can bring back to their institutions.

A key component of professional development is building networks with peers from different types of libraries—public, academic, school—and from various geographic locations. Networking allows for the exchange of ideas across different contexts and fosters collaborations that can lead to groundbreaking projects or services.

Case studies highlighting successful mentor-mentee relationships often reveal increased confidence in mentees' abilities to lead projects or take on new responsibilities within their organizations. Additionally, mentors report a sense of fulfillment in helping shape the next generation of library leaders.

Influential Leaders Shaping Library Futures

The future of libraries is being shaped by influential leaders who are not afraid to challenge traditional paradigms and advocate for transformative change. These individuals understand that libraries must evolve beyond being mere repositories of books into vibrant centers for community engagement, learning, innovation, and cultural preservation.

Influential leaders are characterized by their visionary thinking—seeing potential where others see obstacles—and their commitment to serving diverse communities' needs. They champion initiatives like expanding digital accessibilities such as e-books lending programs or creating makerspaces where patrons can engage with cutting-edge technology like 3D printers.

These leaders also recognize the importance of sustainability in libraries—both environmentally and financially—and work towards implementing practices that ensure long-term viability without compromising service quality or accessibility.

Examples include librarians who have successfully lobbied for increased funding based on demonstrating the library's value as an educational resource or those who have implemented green initiatives reducing waste while promoting environmental awareness among patrons.

To conclude each section:

For further reading on cultivating leadership skills among librarians: - "Developing Library Leaders: A How-To-Do-It Manual For Coaching Team Building And Mentoring Library Staff" by Robert D. Stueart & Maureen Sullivan - "The Accidental Library Leader" by Julie Todaro

For insights into mentorship programs: - "Mentoring & Managing Students in The Academic Library" by Michelle Reale - "The Mentor's Guide: Facilitating Effective Learning Relationships" by Lois J Zachary

On influential leaders shaping library futures: - "Expect More: Demanding Better Libraries For Today's Complex World" by R David Lankes - "Becoming a Library Leader" by Shin Freedman & James Matarazzo

Chapter 12:: : Intellectual Freedom Fighters Worldwide

Global Perspectives on Library Advocacy

Library advocacy has become a global movement, with librarians and information professionals around the world working to promote the value of libraries and their services. This advocacy is not just about securing funding or defending against budget cuts; it's about highlighting the essential role that libraries play in education, democracy, and access to information.

In many parts of the world, libraries are seen as key institutions for advancing literacy, digital inclusion, and lifelong learning. They provide safe spaces for individuals to explore ideas freely without judgment or censorship. Librarians often take on the role of educators and community leaders, teaching digital literacy skills that are crucial in an increasingly online world.

One example of global library advocacy is the work done by IFLA (International Federation of Library Associations and Institutions). IFLA actively promotes the importance of libraries through its various programs and initiatives. It also provides a platform for librarians from different countries to share strategies on how to demonstrate their library's impact on communities.

Another perspective comes from UNESCO's Information for All Programme (IFAP), which focuses on ensuring that all people have access to information they can use to improve their lives. IFAP works with libraries to support knowledge societies where information is freely available and accessible.

However, challenges remain. In some regions, libraries face threats from authoritarian regimes that seek to control access to information. In these cases, library advocacy takes on a more urgent tone as librarians fight against censorship and strive to maintain intellectual freedom.

The push for open access publishing is another area where library advocacy is making waves globally. By supporting open access initiatives, librarians help ensure that scholarly research is available to all, breaking down barriers created by expensive subscription models.

As we look at global perspectives on library advocacy, it becomes clear that while each region may have its unique challenges and cultural contexts, the underlying mission remains consistent: Libraries serve as pillars of free thought and knowledge sharing in society.

Case Studies from Different Continents

Libraries across continents face diverse challenges but share common goals in promoting literacy, providing access to information resources, and serving as community centers. Let's explore case studies from different continents that illustrate how libraries respond uniquely within their socio-political contexts while contributing globally towards intellectual freedom.

In Africa, Kenya's Nairobi National Library serves as a beacon of hope in a country where educational resources are scarce for many citizens. The library has embraced technology by offering e-learning facilities alongside traditional book lending services. It has become instrumental in bridging the digital divide by providing computer training sessions for disadvantaged youth.

Moving over to Asia, South Korea presents an interesting case with its Starfield Library located in Seoul's bustling Coex Mall. This urban library breaks away from conventional norms by being situated inside a shopping mall attracting thousands daily who come not only for books but also cultural events fostering a reading culture among citizens young and old alike.

Europe offers another compelling narrative with Finland's Helsinki Central Library Oodi being hailed as one of the most modern public libraries worldwide. Oodi goes beyond being just a place for books; it includes maker spaces, recording studios, meeting rooms – all designed under principles of openness and accessibility reflecting Finnish values regarding education equality.

In Latin America specifically Brazil São Paulo's Biblioteca de São Paulo stands out through innovative approaches such as sensory storytelling sessions tailored towards visually impaired children thus promoting inclusivity within its community outreach programs.

Lastly North America particularly United States Denver Public Library exemplifies commitment towards social justice issues offering services like social workers onsite assisting homeless patrons addressing societal problems extending far beyond mere book lending duties typical librarian roles entail today.

These case studies demonstrate how despite geographical differences libraries continue evolving adapting local needs while collectively upholding ideals surrounding intellectual freedom worldwide showcasing resilience adaptability inherent within this profession regardless continent they operate upon.

International Collaboration Efforts

The landscape of international collaboration among librarians reflects an understanding that knowledge knows no borders—and neither should efforts to preserve and disseminate it. Collaborative projects span across continents bringing together professionals who share expertise tackle common issues enhance service offerings ultimately benefitting global communities alike.

One notable example Global Libraries initiative funded Bill Melinda Gates Foundation which aimed transform public libraries into engines socioeconomic development provided grants training resources numerous countries helping them leverage power technology meet community needs effectively.

Moreover Electronic Information For Libraries (EIFL) consortium works partnership developing transitioning economy countries facilitate affordable access wide range academic content including research journals databases e-books thereby supporting education innovation scholarship those regions might otherwise be excluded due financial constraints.

Furthermore Program Advancement International Librarianship (PAIL) sponsored American Library Association (ALA) aims build capacity through fostering partnerships between U.S foreign institutions encouraging exchange ideas best practices furthering professional development participants involved.

Additionally International Coalition Digital Preservation (ICDP) brings together organizations dedicated preserving digital heritage ensuring future generations will have same opportunities learn history culture science we do today despite rapid technological changes pose risks loss important data artifacts.

These examples represent just fraction myriad ways which librarians around globe collaborate transcend boundaries create inclusive informed societies harness collective wisdom pool resources tackle grand challenges facing field today tomorrow.

In conclusion whether advocating locally engaging cross-continental projects sharing success stories failures alike international community librarians continues prove itself formidable force championing right free unfettered access knowledge pursuit truth enlightenment betterment humankind everywhere.

Chapter 13:: : Empowering Communities through Knowledge

Tailoring Services to Meet Community Needs

Libraries have long been sanctuaries of knowledge, but in the modern era, they are transforming into dynamic centers that tailor services to meet the specific needs of their communities. This evolution is crucial as it allows libraries to remain relevant and provide meaningful support to their patrons. By conducting community assessments, libraries can identify gaps in services and resources that need addressing. For instance, in areas with a high population of non-English speakers, libraries might offer language classes or bilingual materials.

Moreover, libraries are increasingly becoming technology hubs where people without access to computers or the internet at home can go online. They offer digital literacy programs that help bridge the digital divide, ensuring all community members have the skills necessary to navigate an increasingly digital world. In rural areas, mobile library services extend reach by bringing books and other resources directly to people who might otherwise be isolated due to distance or transportation issues.

One innovative example is the Chicago Public Library's YOUmedia program, which provides teens with a space to explore digital media and develop critical thinking and collaboration skills. This initiative has been replicated in various forms across different libraries, demonstrating how tailored programs can inspire similar efforts elsewhere.

Furthermore, some libraries have adapted their spaces for community use beyond traditional reading areas. They provide meeting rooms for local organizations and host events like job fairs or health screenings that cater directly to community needs. The Queens Library in New York City offers a range of services from legal clinics for immigrants to early childhood education programs.

In essence, by tailoring services and becoming more flexible with their offerings, libraries not only empower individuals but also foster stronger communities through shared knowledge and resources.

Libraries as Catalysts for Social Change

The role of libraries extends far beyond being mere repositories of books; they are active agents of social change within their communities. Librarians serve as frontline workers who engage with diverse populations daily and often witness firsthand the societal challenges these populations face. As such, they are uniquely positioned to initiate programs that address social issues like poverty, illiteracy, and inequality.

Libraries act as catalysts for social change by providing safe spaces where people from all walks of life can come together. They promote inclusivity by offering services tailored for marginalized groups such as refugees or homeless individuals. For example, San Francisco Public Library employs a full-time social worker to assist patrons experiencing homelessness—connecting them with housing resources and support services.

Additionally, many libraries have taken on roles in promoting sustainability practices within their communities through educational workshops on environmental conservation or by implementing green technologies within their own operations. The Austin Public Library's Central Library was awarded LEED Platinum certification for its sustainable design including rainwater collection systems and solar panels.

Another aspect is advocacy; librarians often find themselves advocating for intellectual freedom against censorship attempts or fighting for privacy rights in an age where surveillance is commonplace. They work tirelessly not just within the confines of library walls but also on legislative levels—pushing for policies that ensure equitable access to information.

Success Stories from Around the Globe

Around the globe, there are numerous success stories showcasing how libraries have made significant impacts on their communities through innovative approaches and steadfast dedication.

In Colombia's remote regions plagued by decades-long conflict between government forces and rebel groups—a network known as Biblioburro sees teachers delivering books via donkeys to children who lack access to education facilities. This initiative has brought hope and learning opportunities where there were previously none.

On another continent entirely—the Tūranga Central Library in Christchurch New Zealand played a pivotal role following devastating earthquakes that struck the city in 2010/ 2011.

It became a central point for information dissemination during recovery efforts while also serving as a symbol of resilience—incorporating earthquake-resistant features into its design when it was rebuilt.

In Africa—the Kenya National Library Service operates mobile camel libraries reaching nomadic populations in arid regions where literacy rates are low due largely because schools are scarce or non-existent due these communities' migratory nature; this service brings books directly into hands those who would otherwise be left out educational loop entirely.

These examples illustrate just how versatile modern-day librarians must be —they're educators activists technologists cultural stewards all rolled into one profession whose impact stretches far beyond what one might traditionally expect from local library staff member; they truly embody heroism our time ensuring truth prevails over noise every corner planet we call home. For further reading on these topics consider "Palaces for the People" by Eric Klinenberg which explores how social infrastructure like libraries can help forge stronger more cohesive societies "Bibliotech: Why Libraries Matter More Than Ever In Age Of Google" John Palfrey which argues importance maintaining robust public library systems digital age "The Bad-Ass Librarians Timbuktu" Joshua Hammer tells true story group librarians risked lives save ancient manuscripts Al Qaeda occupation Mali each book offers unique perspective power potential library institutions today's world conclude it clear that whether providing tailored services acting catalysts social change celebrating success stories around globe continue play vital role empowering communities through knowledge understanding compassion times uncertainty challenge celebration alike

Chapter 14:: : Future Trends Impacting Libraries

Anticipating Changes in Information Consumption

As we look towards the future, anticipating changes in information consumption is crucial for libraries to remain relevant and effective. The digital age has already transformed how people access and interact with information, and this evolution continues at a rapid pace. One significant trend is the increasing preference for multimedia content over traditional text-based resources. Libraries must adapt by offering a broader range of formats, including video, audio, and interactive media.

The rise of artificial intelligence (AI) and machine learning algorithms will further change information consumption patterns. AI can personalize content discovery, making it easier for users to find materials that match their interests and learning styles. Libraries will need to integrate these technologies into their catalog systems to provide more tailored recommendations.

Another aspect of changing information consumption is the growing importance of data literacy. As society becomes more data-driven, libraries must offer resources and training that help patrons understand and analyze data effectively. This includes providing access to databases, statistical tools, and educational programs focused on data skills.

Moreover, the concept of "information on demand" is becoming increasingly prevalent. Users expect instant access to information anytime and anywhere. Libraries must invest in robust digital infrastructures that support e-books, online journals, streaming services, and remote access to library resources.

In response to these trends, libraries should also consider partnerships with other institutions such as schools, universities, businesses, and technology companies. These collaborations can enhance resource offerings and ensure that libraries are at the forefront of technological advancements in information delivery.

Preparing for the Next Wave of Digital Innovations

Libraries have always been early adopters of new technologies that facilitate access to knowledge. As we prepare for the next wave of digital innovations, it's essential for libraries to stay ahead by embracing emerging technologies that can transform service delivery.

One area where digital innovation will have a profound impact is augmented reality (AR) and virtual reality (VR). These technologies can create immersive learning experiences for patrons. For example, AR could bring historical events to life within the library space or allow users to explore complex scientific concepts through interactive simulations.

Blockchain technology also presents opportunities for libraries in terms of secure record-keeping and sharing digital assets without intermediaries. It could revolutionize how libraries manage copyrights and user privacy while facilitating a new level of collaboration between institutions.

The Internet of Things (IoT) offers another avenue for innovation within libraries by connecting physical spaces with digital services. Smart shelves equipped with RFID tags not only streamline inventory management but also enhance user experience by helping patrons locate materials more efficiently.

Furthermore, as voice-activated assistants become more sophisticated, they could serve as virtual librarians—assisting with queries or navigating library databases through natural language processing.

To capitalize on these innovations, continuous professional development for library staff is imperative. Training programs should focus on building technical skills required to implement and maintain new technologies while fostering an innovative mindset among staff members.

Strategic Planning for Future Challenges

Strategic planning is vital for libraries facing an array of future challenges ranging from budget constraints to shifts in public perception about their relevance in a digital world. A proactive approach involves identifying potential obstacles ahead while crafting flexible strategies that allow adaptation as circumstances change.

One challenge is ensuring equitable access to technology across diverse communities served by libraries. As resources shift online or become digitized exclusively, there's a risk of widening the digital divide if certain populations lack necessary tools or skills needed for access. Libraries must advocate for policies supporting universal broadband access while providing training programs aimed at improving digital literacy among underserved groups.

Another challenge lies in maintaining physical collections amidst space limitations and funding pressures favoring electronic resources. Strategic planning here might involve reevaluating collection development policies or exploring off-site storage solutions coupled with efficient retrieval systems ensuring timely patron access when needed.

Additionally, privacy concerns are escalating as surveillance capitalism grows pervasive within society; thus safeguarding patron data becomes ever more critical within strategic planning efforts undertaken by libraries today seeking trustworthiness tomorrow's landscape dominated by privacy issues surrounding personal information usage online environments alike .

Finally , sustainability initiatives represent both ethical imperatives environmental necessities which require incorporation into long-term plans . From reducing energy consumption via green building designs implementing recycling programs promoting sustainable practices amongst patrons themselves , every aspect operations should reflect commitment preserving planet future generations enjoy same benefits current ones do today .

In conclusion , each area discussed represents just fraction considerations facing modern-day librarianship ; however , they underscore importance agility foresight profession continually evolving meet needs its community . For those interested delving deeper into topics presented here suggested readings include "The Atlas New Librarianship" R David Lankes "Library 2020: Today's Leading Visionaries Describe Tomorrow's Library" edited Joseph Janes provide comprehensive insights into ongoing transformations shaping field .

Chapter 15:: : Marketing Library Services Effectively

Creating a Brand Identity for Your Library

In the realm of library services, establishing a brand identity is not merely about aesthetics; it's about crafting a narrative that resonates with the community and distinguishes the institution in a crowded informational landscape. A compelling brand identity for a library involves an amalgamation of visual elements, such as logos and color schemes, and intangible aspects like mission statements and service philosophies that collectively communicate the library's unique value proposition.

To create this identity, libraries must first understand their patrons' needs and perceptions. Engaging with community members through surveys, focus groups, and informal conversations can yield insights into what they cherish about library services and what gaps need to be bridged. With this knowledge, libraries can tailor their branding to highlight programs that align with community interests—be it children's reading initiatives or digital literacy workshops.

Moreover, libraries should consider partnerships with local businesses and organizations to enhance their brand visibility. For instance, co-hosting events or creating joint campaigns can introduce the library to new audiences while reinforcing its role as a community pillar.

A case study worth examining is the rebranding of the Toronto Public Library. By adopting a more modern logo and launching targeted campaigns around user stories, they managed to increase public engagement significantly. Their "Human Library" event series where patrons could 'check out' people with unique life experiences for conversations was particularly effective in humanizing their brand.

Utilizing Social Media Platforms to Reach Out to Patrons

Social media platforms offer libraries unprecedented opportunities to connect with patrons beyond physical walls. To leverage these platforms effectively, libraries must adopt strategies tailored to each platform's strengths and audience demographics.

For example, Instagram can showcase visually appealing content such as new arrivals or behind-the-scenes glimpses into library operations. Twitter serves well for real-time updates on events or sharing thought-provoking articles related to literacy and culture. Facebook groups can foster community discussions around book recommendations or library programs.

Libraries should also explore emerging platforms popular among younger demographics to stay relevant. TikTok campaigns featuring staff book talks or literary challenges can engage teens who might not be reached through traditional marketing channels.

The New York Public Library's use of Instagram Stories to publish animated versions of classic novels like "Alice in Wonderland" exemplifies innovative social media use that both entertains and educates followers.

Effective Outreach Strategies to Increase Engagement

Outreach strategies are crucial for increasing engagement with library services. Libraries must go beyond passive communication by actively seeking opportunities for interaction within their communities.

One effective strategy is mobile outreach services—bookmobiles or pop-up libraries at local festivals—that bring resources directly to people who may not visit physical branches. Another approach is offering expertise at non-library events; librarians could conduct information literacy workshops at schools or participate in local business expos.

Collaborative programs with schools can also bolster engagement while supporting educational goals. For instance, summer reading challenges co-sponsored by libraries and school districts encourage continued learning during vacation months while fostering a love for reading among students.

The Seattle Public Library's partnership with local coffee shops where baristas recommend books curated by librarians demonstrates how outreach can creatively intersect with everyday life in unexpected places.

Measuring Impact and Demonstrating Value

Quantifying the impact of library services is essential for demonstrating value to stakeholders such as funders or governing bodies. Traditional metrics like circulation numbers or program attendance are important but do not capture the full scope of a library's influence on individual lives and communities.

To address this gap, libraries are increasingly adopting outcome-based evaluation methods that assess changes in knowledge, behavior, skills, status, or condition attributable to library services. Surveys that measure improvements in digital literacy after attending computer classes at the library provide concrete evidence of impact beyond mere participation rates.

Furthermore, storytelling can be an impactful tool for illustrating value qualitatively. Collecting patron testimonials about how access to certain resources has transformed their lives offers compelling narratives that statistics alone cannot convey.

The Sacramento Public Library's annual report includes data-driven infographics alongside personal stories from patrons affected by various programs—a blend that powerfully communicates both quantitative impact and qualitative outcomes.

Title: "The Super Librarians and The Trial of Fury"

Synopsis:

"The Super Librarians and The Trial of Fury" is an enlightening non-fiction book that redefines the image of librarians in the modern era. Far from being mere custodians of books, librarians emerge as valiant warriors against the onslaught of misinformation and digital chaos. This book takes readers on a journey through the transformative role librarians play in society, showcasing their real-world heroism as they combat cognitive biases, digital fury, and the spread of false information.

Through vivid narratives and engaging case studies, the book reveals how these unsung heroes use their research prowess and fact-checking expertise to uphold truth and accuracy. It delves into their commitment to literacy promotion, historical preservation, and their skillful navigation of emotional neutrality when confronted with challenging patrons.

As it explores the multifaceted aspects of librarian heroism, "The Super Librarians and The Trial of Fury" also tackles ethical dilemmas such as access to information versus protection from harmful content. It illustrates how librarians are equipped with training to handle these complex issues with grace and professionalism.

In an age where libraries have evolved into dynamic community centers, this book highlights how librarians have embraced technological advancements to redefine their roles within our ever-changing digital landscape. It underscores the resilience and adaptability required for librarians to remain relevant and effective in their mission.

Intended for a broad audience including educators, policymakers, students, or anyone curious about the pivotal role knowledge keepers play behind the scenes, this book offers a fresh perspective on a profession that profoundly shapes society in quiet yet significant ways.

"The Super Librarians and The Trial of Fury" is not only a celebration of intellectual freedom fighters around the globe but also an affirmation of libraries as steadfast guardians of knowledge. Through a blend of storytelling, empirical evidence, and expert insights, readers will come away with a renewed respect for those who tirelessly work to ensure that truth triumphs over noise in our communities.